Looking *at* Pictures

Making Faces

~ Joy Richardson ~

FRANKLIN WATTS
LONDON • SYDNEY

C56 0000 0410 069

WREXHAM LIBRARY AND INFO SERVICES

C56410069	
Bertrams	24.11.07
J757	£5.99
WR BO	R

© 1997 Franklin Watts

First published in Great Britain in 1997

Franklin Watts
96 Leonard Street
London EC2A 4RH

Franklin Watts Australia
14 Mars Road
Lane Cove
NSW 2066

0 7496 3568 1

10 9 8 7 6 5

Dewey Decimal Classification Number: 757

A CIP catalogue record for this book is
available from the British Library.

Editor: Sarah Ridley
Designer: Louise Thomas
Art Director: Robert Walster

Photographs:
Copyright British Museum/Reg. no. 13595 pgs 4-5, pg 30 (detail); copyright
photo RMN/L'ete/Archimboldo pgs 10-11, RMN/The Cheat Holding the Ace of
Diamonds/La Tour pgs 14-15, pg 28 (detail), RMN/Doctor Paul Gachet/van Gogh pgs
22-23; reproduced by courtesy of the Trustees, National Gallery, London
Ghirlandaio/Portrait of a Girl cover, pgs 6-7, pg 27 (detail), Cranach/Portraits of
Johann the Steadfast and Johann Friedrich the Magnanimous pgs 8-9,
Champaigne/Triple Portrait of Cardinal Richelieu pgs 12-13, pg 27 (detail), pg 29
(detail), Chardin/The Young Schoolmistress pgs 16-17, Hogarth/The Graham Children
pgs 18-19, pg 28 (detail), Le Brun/Self-Portrait in a Straw Hat pgs 20-21, pg 31 (detail);
Succession Picasso/DACS 1997 Weeping Woman, Pablo Picasso/copyright Tate Gallery,
London pgs 24-25.

Printed in Belgium

Contents

What shape are faces?
How do you make a nose stand out?
What colour is skin?
What makes a face look sad?

Read on to enjoy some of the faces created by painters in the past.

Portrait on a Roman Mummy

This face looks out from the
mummy of a young boy
who lived in Roman times.

He has a wide round forehead and a pointed chin.

Light glints in his eye beneath the spiky eyelashes.

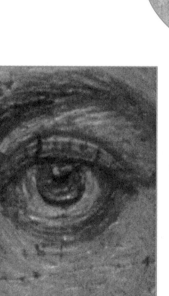

Eyebrow arches lead down to his nose.

Dark dabs make the nostrils.

Portrait of a Girl
painted by Ghirlandaio

This girl was growing up five hundred years ago.
The picture remembers her for ever.

What colour is her skin?

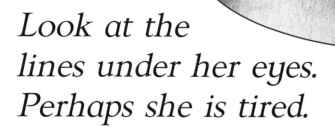

Look at the
lines under her eyes.
Perhaps she is tired.

Can you see the light
shining on her hair?

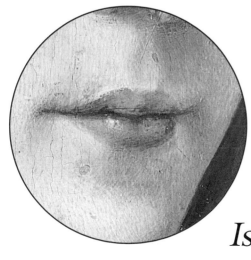

Is she smiling?

Father and Son
painted by Cranach

The man is an important ruler.
His six-year-old son looks grand
in his best clothes.

Do you think the boy looks like his father?

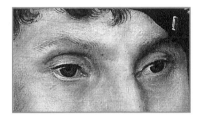 Look how these
eyes look older
than these eyes.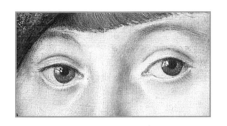

The boy's face
is framed by a
very fine hat.

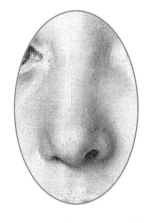 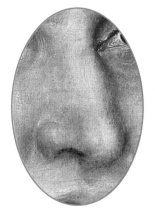

Whose nose is whose?
Look how the shading makes the noses stand out.

Summer
painted by Archimboldo

The painter makes Summer
from a face full of fruits and vegetables.

The peas in the pod are
teeth for eating.
Look for the cherry lips.

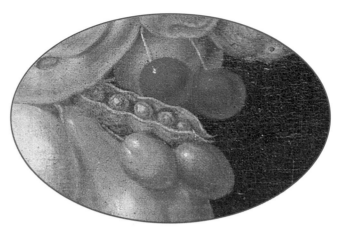

Can you find the eye,
the eyelids and the eyebrow?

The peach
rounds out a
bulging cheek.

What do these stand for?

Triple Portrait of
Cardinal Richelieu
painted by Champaigne

The painter shows the same man
from the front and from each side,
all in the same picture.

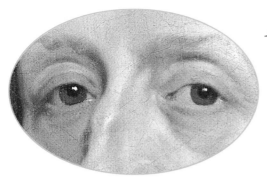

His brown eyes gaze
wisely at you.
See how they look
from the side.

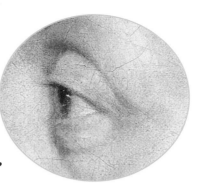

Look at his tidy moustache
and his shaved skin.

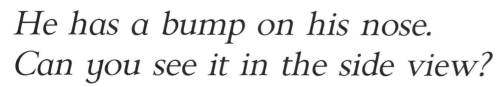

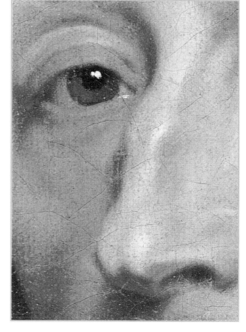

He has a bump on his nose.
Can you see it in the side view?

Look to see if both sides of
his face are exactly the same.

The Cheat Holding the Ace of Diamonds
painted by La Tour

Someone is cheating
with cards behind his back.
Do the others know what is going on?

No-one is saying anything.
Look at all the closed mouths.

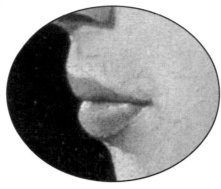

Look at the face shapes.
This one is oval like an
egg. Follow the eyes to see
where they are looking.

Light and shade fall
on the faces.
Where is the light
coming from?

The Young Schoolmistress
painted by Chardin

The big girl points to the letters.
The young child is trying to read.

Look at the expression on each face. One says "This is easy." One says, "This is hard."

Where are their eyes looking?

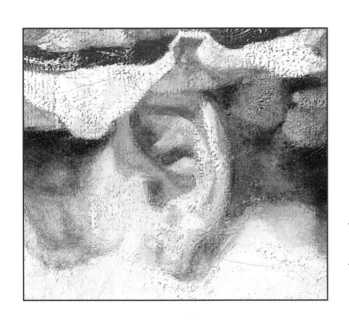

The big girl's face is shown from the side. You can see her whole ear.

Can you find these colours in their cheeks?

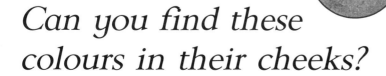

The Graham Children
painted by Hogarth

The portrait shows off
the children in their best clothes.
Can you see the family likeness?

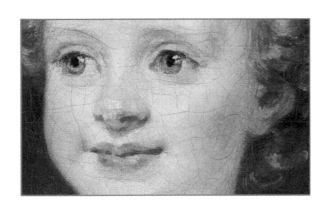

Each face is slightly turned.
How many ears are in sight?

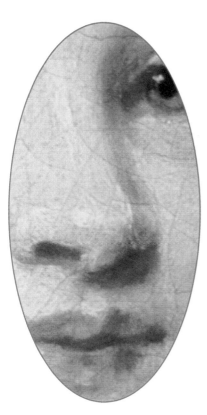

Look at the
face shapes.
Are they alike?

How are the noses painted
to make them stand out?

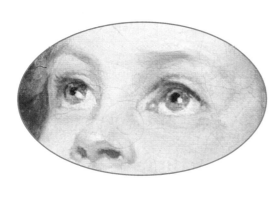

What are these
eyes looking at?

Self-Portrait
painted by Le Brun

This is a self-portrait.
The painter must have looked hard
at herself in a mirror.

Look at the colours on her palette.

Which colours does
she use for
her hair ...

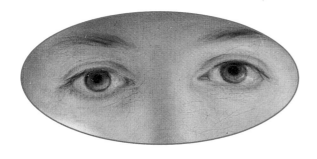

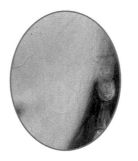

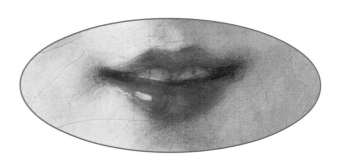

her eyes ...   her skin ...   her mouth?

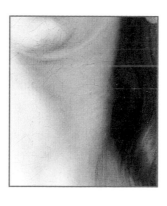

How does she
make the shadows
on her skin?

Doctor Paul Gachet
painted by van Gogh

Van Gogh painted his friend the doctor.
He knew him well.

Look at the piercing blue eyes.

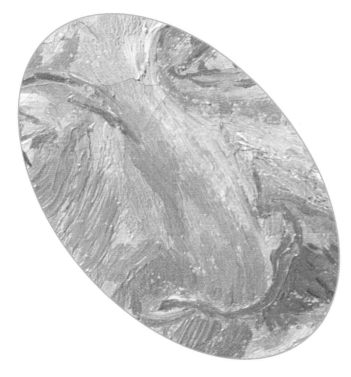

Follow the long nose
down to the pale lips.

He has a thoughtful look with
knuckles pressed into his cheek.

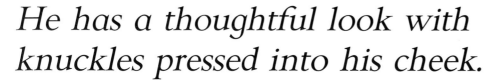

Black lines mark out
his cap and bushy hair.

Weeping Woman
painted by Picasso

The woman has smart hair
and a bright hat but she is feeling very sad.

Can you see startled eyebrows ...

tears coming out of her eyes ...

jagged lines around her crying mouth ...

fingers gripping a handkerchief?

The colours show her feelings too.
Look at the cold white, the sour
yellow and all the thick black lines.

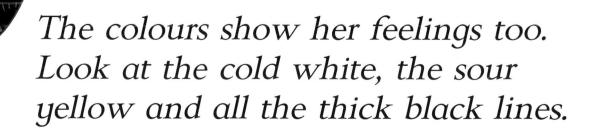

Making Faces Yourself

Skin colours

Skin is not really white, or brown, or black.
You have to look closely to see the real
colour. Your cheeks may even be a slightly
different colour from your neck and hands.

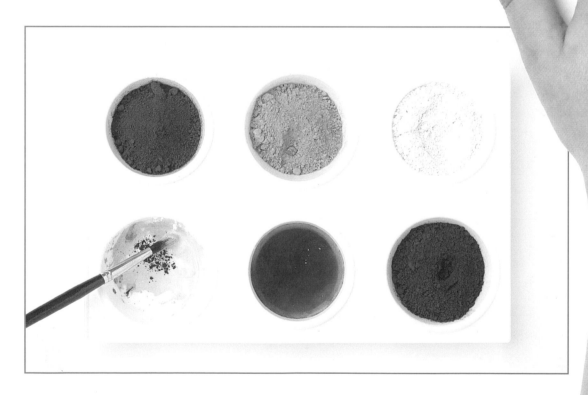

Try mixing paint to match the colour of your skin.

For help, look back at page 16.

Painting hair

You cannot paint every hair on your head, but try using brush strokes to show straight hair, curly hair, smooth hair or springy hair.

For help, look back at page 6.

Use a lighter shade to show where the hair catches the light.

Showing noses

Noses are easier from the side than from the front. Try painting the same nose both ways.

For help, look back at pages 12 and 14.

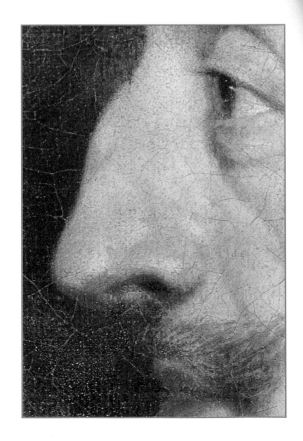

Face shapes

What shape is a face? Look through this book and at people around you. How many different face shapes can you find?

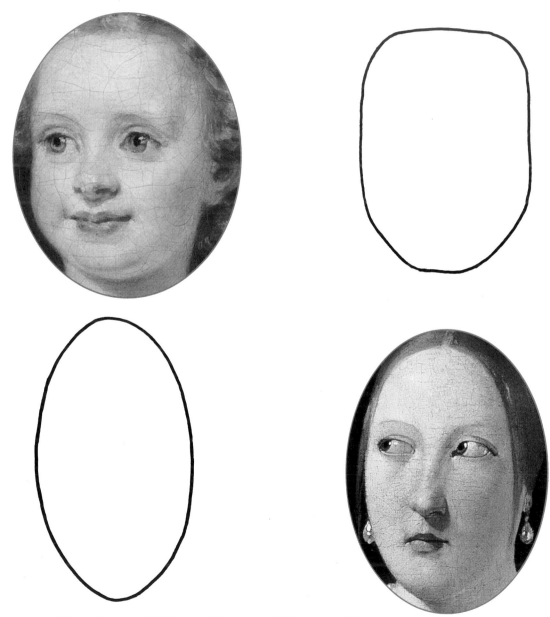

Try making a collection of face shapes. Draw the outline of each face shape and mark in the eyes and mouth.

For help, look back at page 20.

Faces and feelings

Pull a happy face, a sad face, or a surprised face in the mirror. Now paint your expression, choosing colours and shapes to match the feeling.

For help, look back at page 24.

Turning heads

Faces can be painted from the front, from the side, or anywhere in between. Try painting the same face from different angles.

For help, look back at page 12.

More about the pictures in this book

■ Portrait on a Roman mummy of a Boy

The boy died in the first century A.D. His body was treated and wrapped in bandages to preserve it for the afterlife. His face was painted on a wooden panel, with coloured wax, to decorate the head of the mummy and to keep his eyes open on the world.

■ Portrait of a Girl

Domenico Ghirlandaio (about 1448-1494) set up a studio in Florence with his brothers and other painters. He was often asked to make paintings for churches and wealthy people. This portrait was made in his studio, (about 1490 judging by the hair style), but we are not sure who painted it, or who the girl was.

■ Portraits of Johann the Steadfast and Johann Friedrich the Magnanimous

Lucas Cranach (1472-1553) was a German painter. He painted this father-and-son portrait in 1509. Johann Steadfast was the Elector of Saxony. His son, Johann Friedrich, who was six in this painting, later succeeded his father as ruler. Young Johann could not be painted with his mother as would have been more usual: she had died giving birth to him.

■ Summer

Guiseppe Archimboldo (1527-1593) was Italian, but he worked at the royal court in Prague. He created curious, entertaining pictures by constructing characters from plants and animals. 'Summer' is one of four paintings representing the seasons. 'Autumn', 'Winter' and 'Spring' also have heads created from fruits, vegetables, leaves and bits of wood.

■ Triple Portrait of Cardinal Richelieu

Philippe de Champaigne (1602-1674) was the best portrait painter of his time in France. The King's powerful minister, Cardinal Richelieu, asked him to paint this all-round portrait. It was then sent to Rome to guide a sculptor who was working on a statue of the famous man. Champaigne even wrote helpfully above the face on the right that this was the best likeness.

■ The Cheat Holding the Ace of Diamonds

Georges de la Tour (1593-1652) was a French painter. He painted ordinary-looking scenes and filled them with hidden meanings, using dramatic lighting to add to the air of mystery. In this painting, the three on the left seem to be secretly in league against the young man on the right.

■ The Young Schoolmistress

Jean Siméon Chardin (1699-1779) was a very successful painter of still life and everyday scenes. He loved painting children, not posing for a portrait, but caught up in their own activities: spinning a top; blowing bubbles; playing school. He wanted to show how they felt and thought as well as what they looked like.

■ The Graham Children

William Hogarth (1697-1764) was a British painter. He started as an engraver and this painting was his first successful large-group portrait. Among the shining, smiling faces, the cat eyeing the bird is a reminder of death. In fact, the youngest child, Thomas, died before the portrait was completed.

■ Self-Portrait in a Straw Hat

Elizabeth Vigée Le Brun (1755-1842) was witty, charming and beautiful. She often painted the Queen of France and her children before the French Revolution. She took the pose for this self-portrait from 'The Straw Hat', a painting by Rubens which she especially admired.

■ Doctor Paul Gachet

Vincent van Gogh (1853-1890) was born in Holland, but lived in France from 1886. He spent the last few months of his life at Auvers, painting almost a picture a day. He often painted Dr. Paul Gachet who looked after him there and became a good friend.

■ Weeping Woman

Pablo Picasso (1881-1973) was Spanish. In 1936 the Spanish Civil War broke out. In 1937, Picasso painted 'Guernica' to show the suffering caused by the war. He carried on thinking about sadness and in the next few months he painted a whole series of pictures of weeping women. This is the last one he made.

Index